Muslim Women in Western Society

KHADIJA MAREEF

WOW Book Publishing™

Muslim Women in Western Society

Copyright © 2020 Khadija Mareef

ISBN: 978-1-716-41588-3

All rights reserved. No portion of this book may be reproduced mechanically, electronically, or by any other means, including photocopying, without permission of the publisher or author except in the case of brief quotations embodied in critical articles and reviews. It is illegal to copy this book, post it to a website, or distribute it by any other means without permission from the publisher or author.

Limits of Liability and Disclaimer of Warranty

The author and publisher shall not be liable for your misuse of the enclosed material. This book is strictly for informational and educational purposes only.

Warning – Disclaimer

The purpose of this book is to educate and entertain. The author and/or publisher do not guarantee that anyone following these techniques, suggestions, tips, ideas, or strategies will become successful. The author and/or publisher shall have neither liability nor responsibility to anyone with respect to any loss or damage caused, or alleged to be caused, directly or indirectly by the information contained in this book.

Publisher
10-10-10 Publishing
Markham, ON
Canada

Printed in Canada and the United States of America

Dedication

I wrote this book to every immigrant woman living overseas who is struggling to fit in with the new culture, speak up about their rights, and, specifically, be themselves. I dedicate this to everyone who wants to know about the experiences of Muslim women in daily life and how these experiences affect their personal, emotional, and professional life.

Love,
Khadija Zegdi

Table of Contents

Testimonials	vii
About the Author	ix
Foreword	xi
Acknowledgements	xiii
Life in Western Society	1
Lifestyle in UK	3
People	6
Cultural diversity	9
Freedom	12
Opportunities	15
Quality life	18
9/11 Consequences	23
Blames and Shames	26
Mainstream Media	29
Fear	35
Judging the Book by the Cover	38
Low Self-esteem	46

Judgement Clouds the Mind	49
Discrimination/Depression	52
The Importance of Having Support	55
Role of Friends	58
Colleagues	62
Media	68
Importance of Integration	73
Learn the Language	76
Get Involved within the Community	79
Start Working	83
Be Inspirational	86
Build Mental & Emotional Strength	89
Help Others	93
The Truth of Islam	95
Tolerance	98
Respecting others	100
Take Care and Be Kind	103
My Journey to Self-Confidence	106
Self-Care	108
Think Positive	111
Set Small Goals to Achieve	114
Be Grateful	117
Empower Yourself with Knowledge	120
Have a Vision for Your Dream	124

Testimonials

"Khadija helped me so much when I was very depressed and upset at work due to the way my manager treated me. She is the best person to give advice, and I recommend her book for reading."

-Ella, Business Developer

"This book contains a very important message to all women in general and to Muslim women in specific. Khadija truly wants you to know it and apply it too."

-Betty, Treasurer

"My friend, Khadija, is a special person with a big heart. She gives help and support without asking for something in return. Her assistance was highly appreciated while she was living in Morocco. I would recommend her book for sure."

-Karima, Accountant, Morocco

"I would strongly advise you to read Khadija's book. She is sharing her experience with you in a smooth way that might be a very useful guide for any women planning to move overseas."

-Jay, Account Executive

"If you're not sure about how your life is going to be after moving abroad, Khadija's book will give you an insight about the true life and how can you deal with any day to day problem."

-Joyce, England

"Being a powerful woman is not an easy character trait to develop, especially if you are living overseas, are struggling to get integrated, and find your way within the new culture. This book includes amazing speeches that will be very useful to you."

-Claire, France

"Growing up as a woman wasn't easy for me, especially with all the problems I had since I came to Spain. Khadija describes it all and gives us, as women, a powerful message to stand up for ourselves."

-Samia, Tunisia

About the Author

Khadija is a Moroccan woman living with her small family in Buckinghamshire, England. She is a strong woman, full of energy, dedication, and inspiration who is trying to spread her motivational speeches as a message of hope and peace around the world. Khadija wrote this book to express and demonstrate the struggle and challenges that a Muslim woman faces on daily basis, which feels the need to clarify issues and solutions. The nature of her job allows her to travel and discover many European countries where she experienced various interactions (both good and bad) from different cultures. Khadija's book is all about her experiences and serves as a message of empowerment to all the women in her situation. She has done this, so they can express themselves and fulfil their life. Find more inspirational and empowerment talks from Khadija at https://www.facebook.com/Inspire-with-Khadija

Foreword

Dear Reader,

You need to grab hold of this book, especially if you are a woman moving from your home to a new culture overseas, struggling to find a balance between your religion and the modern lifestyle. Khadija shares her experiences of different situations within many cultures and gives you, the reader, an insight into the true life of a Muslim woman in Western society. The knowledge in this book has the power to help you create solid and powerful personality traits, which will help you truly change your life and move forward. From my long experience in this industry, I can tell you that Khadija has the desire, spirit, and dedication to help you overcome your problems and be a better version of your professional and inspirational self.

-Vishal Morjaria
International Speaker and
Award-Winning Author

Acknowledgements

I acknowledge the souls that are no longer here, such as our Prophet Muhammed (*"peace be upon him"*) and my parents. Their inspiration still fuels me every day. I'm grateful for the leadership of his Majesty the King of Morocco, Mohamed VI, her Majesty, the Queen of England, Michelle Obama, Oprah Winfrey, Mel Robbins, and many others who I've not named but who continue to tirelessly help make the world a better place. I acknowledge some of the great business minds that inspired me through my journey. I've had the pleasure of learning from their amazing speeches and presentations, such as Les Brown, Vishal Morjata, Dan Peena, Jim Rohn, Warren Buffet, and Tony Robbins. Importantly, I acknowledge my husband for his unlimited help and support in the process of writing this book, as well as being by my side during this journey. Finally, I acknowledge you, the reader, for receiving this book and using it in the most positive way that you know.

Life in Western Society

"Believe in free will. Of those that, like us, are in a privileged situation at least. For you, for me: people who are living in western society, people who are not repressed, who are free. We can choose. The things go largely like you want them to go. You control your own life. Your own will is extremely powerful."

-J. K. Rowling

I would like to give my readers an insight into the reason why I choose to write this book and how the idea became a reality. I came from Morocco, a North African country that most people call "the gateway to Africa" (there is just 14km between it and Spain). My childhood was peaceful and normal as all kids in my age group, though I grew up without a father, who died when I was 5 years old. I never had any issues with anybody, and I was always successful in school and university, where I got my bachelor's degree in auditing and management control. Suddenly, the challenge started when I lost one of the pillars of my family: my mum. This happened in my last year of university, which was very hard for me to cope with on top of studying and looking after my brothers and myself. Thanks God, I was lucky enough to find my husband. At the time, he was a friend who assisted me gradually to overcome the situation, and supported me to focus on my studies, as he knew this would lead to success. He was right, and after getting my degree, I started training as a professional accountant until I found a job. After that, I got married to my beloved husband and then I moved to the UK. This is where my journey begins.

Lifestyle in UK

When I was in Morocco, I never thought that I would end up living the rest of my life in a different country. I liked the warm weather in my hometown, Agadir. I enjoyed the smell of fresh food every day and being around family and friends. Moving to England after I got married was an immense change in my life. I left all of my memories and souvenirs behind in Morocco and started a new journey, full of surprises and challenges in the UK. Thanks God my husband was with me at every step, guiding and supporting me through the difficult moments. It wasn't easy for me to accept the transformation of my life from one country to another, and familiarising myself with the rules, laws, and culture was challenging at times. The first time I arrived in England, I was fascinated with the landscape and the parks; this was something I was missing from Agadir. I spent most of the weeks walking or running in parks and enjoying the fresh air.

My husband started taking me to the nearby towns and cities to get to know the culture. I liked Oxford with the amazing English history and architecture style, Liverpool, the hometown of The Beatles, where River Mersey meets the Irish Sea, and many more amazing and interesting places. I feel very lucky to have a husband who was trying to provide me with as much information as he could so that I could gain confidence and be able to live a normal life, comfortably, and without negativity. I felt very supported in the UK compared to other women who struggle to find the necessary support and guidance. These two things allow women to feel comfortable in a country that is completely different from their home, in a country where the culture is extremely unlike what they grew up with, in a country where freedom means everything. I would advise any woman who struggles to find her way while living abroad to try and seek support from your family; they are the first ones who can understand your situation more than anyone else.

If you don't feel like sharing your feelings and thoughts with your close ones, then your friends are most likely to help, especially if they come from different cultures. They might understand you more and change their thoughts about you and your culture. For more support and assistance, visit my page below where you can chat and connect with other women living in the same situation. I'm sure you will find it very helpful in all sorts of situations. Facebook link: https://www.facebook.com/Inspire-with-Khadija

People

"There is a Story behind every person, there is a reason why they are the way they are. Think about that and respect them for who they are."

-Marcandangel

The interesting thing I've noticed in UK is that some people will just judge you without knowing you. Like the proverb says, "Don't judge a book by its cover." To be honest, it's true. We don't know what is behind the cover until we start reading the book. The same principle applies to people. How can you make a judgment without giving another person a chance to express him or herself by talking, writing, or acting? The UK is a rich society in terms of the number of cultures living together. There is a mixture of immigrants coming from worldwide, making the UK more interesting and amazing to discover.

My first assumption was that it would be a great opportunity to learn from each other, help each other, and support each other. Unfortunately, this doesn't apply to everyone as I had many bad experiences where people, especially from eastern Europe, were very nasty to me. They looked at me like I had two heads or had been mean to them, even though I hadn't done anything to them. To be honest, it hurt me in the beginning; after a certain period, I've learned it as lack of exposure to other cultures. They're probably not used to travelling to any of the Islamic countries or never had a chance to work with someone who is Muslim, which, I believe, explains their behaviour. On the other hand, I worked with some amazing people, and I'm still in contact with them now due to their help and support.

In my first job, I used to start early (7:30 am), and I wasn't driving at that time. My husband couldn't take me because my stepson was 5 years old and couldn't be left on his own. Thank God one of my colleagues, Stephan, who lives in the same town, offered to pick me up and drop me back whenever he was around. He was Jewish, which might surprise you. How can a Jewish person give a lift to a Muslim woman? Well, he did, and I'm so grateful to him as he never got fed up of picking me up or dropping me back. Every day, we would meet with a big smile and talk about different subjects without any issues or sensitivity. He saved me money and time; the bus usually takes more than 2 hours each way, which was exhausting. Our friendship was based on respect. Each one of us respected the other's opinion, religion, and feedback. This is how it should be, in my opinion.

Why do we think we are better than others? It's not true, in my opinion. I believe in equality, and we are all the same. It doesn't matter the colour of skin, the culture, the gender, or the religion. You, the reader of my book, should spread this message around your own environment. Take the lead, and be the messenger of peace. It is essential to make changes and build a society based on respect and peace, which allows us all to have a better future.

Cultural diversity

"We need to help students and parents cherish and preserve the ethic and cultural diversity that nourishes and strengthens this community – and this nation."

-Cesar Chavez

It is interesting the number of the cultures living together in the UK. It shows the level of the tolerance and peace in this country. When I moved to the UK, I thought I would only be meeting English people, but I was wrong. I was shocked by the diversity and mixture of cultures. The most interesting thing is the areas that symbolize each community. Chinatown, for example, is an ethnic enclave in Westminster. It contains several Chinese bakeries, restaurants, souvenir shops, supermarkets, and Chinese-run businesses. I liked all the decorations in the area, especially during

Chinese New Year as it's so colourful and bright. I used to go there with my husband, eating in the buffet restaurant. Banglatown is an area in London well known by its large community of Bangladeshi people. It's a vibrant place where you can experience all sort of curry dishes.

Southall, or Little India as they call it, is a large suburban district of West London. Many products are sold there, including jewellery, spices, and sari, which is an expensive material worn by Indian women. It's a busy place, and very crowded, which demonstrates real life in India. All the places listed above are just a drop in the ocean compared to other parts of the UK where you would be able to try foods, beverages, and sweets from all over the world without leaving the country. If you have the chance to be in the UK, don't forget to make the most of it by going to these places and trying all sorts of foods and drinks. This is the only place where you can meet the world.

Being part of this culture allowed me to be exposed to different traditions and learn from them as well as others learning from mine. Since not many people were able to travel to Morocco, I used to cook some of our famous foods, like Tajine or couscous, and take it with me to work to share it with my colleagues. Their first impression was that it was very delicious. These dishes combine spices and flavours that you might never have tried. Some of them asked for recipes to make it at home. I remember one lady, who used to be my neighbour, said a sentence that I'll never forget. She said: "I don't have money to travel abroad and see the world, but thank God I live in the UK so the whole world comes to me." She was right. If you don't have money to book fancy holidays and discover new places, you can see the world from where you are and enjoy it.

Freedom

"Freedom is the Oxygen of the soul."
                              -Moshe Dayan

One of the most amazing things in UK is freedom, and the best place to see it is London. London is considered to be one of the most important global cities in the world and has been termed the most powerful, most influential, most desirable, , most expensive, most visited, sustainable innovative, most investment friendly, and most popular for work city in the world. It has a large diversity of people and cultures, and more than 300 languages are spoken in the region. So amazing. Its so vibrant it's a live city.

As indicated on Google

If you are a tourist in London or you are living there, you would be amazed by the mixture of cultures and diversity of peoples. Everyone looks different. You can see hairs coloured in purple, red, orange, or blue; it's like a rainbow all over the place, dressing up differently. Most follow the trend with holes in jeans, T-shirts, shirts, jumpers, skirts, and dresses. You cannot imagine how people dress up; it's just amazing because this represents the level of freedom and respect in this culture. My memories brought me back when I just moved to UK; I was a shy girl, lacking confidence because I didn't speak fluent English and my accent was more French than Arabic. I had a bad experience with some people where they thought they were better than me just because I was wearing a scarf, didn't speak the language, or didn't have enough confidence to defend myself. You might be in the same place where I was years ago, and you are still suffering internally, unable to speak up due to a lack of support. I'm advising you to stand up for yourself and stop any kind of abuse; no one allowed to treat you badly due to your colour, culture, or faith.

No one has the right to treat you badly. You have the right to go out, you have the right to eat out, you have the right to go shopping, and you have the right to do whatever you want whenever you want as long as you don't hurt others. There are good people too, though; I still remember some nice people who were working with me and who were very understanding about how difficult adjusting to new a culture could be. They tried to make me feel more like I was home and among my family rather than strangers. They invited me to their weddings, birthdays, leaving dos, and more where I discovered and learned more about the British culture. This made it easier for me to be more involved and become integrated in this society.

Opportunities

"We will never be able to recognize opportunities if we first don't recognize all that we have and all that we've been given."

-Joel Osteen

Compared to any other country, I believe any person living in UK have more chances to succeed and reach his/her goals than anybody living anywhere else. You going to say why is that? I simply reply that I lived in Morocco, and I do have friends worldwide as well. We been talking about how much time and effort it would take us to achieve our dreams back home compared to UK. The society here is helping anybody; it doesn't matter your background, doesn't matter your origins, doesn't matter your colour, doesn't matter your style, doesn't matter your religion as long as you got a dream, you've got a vison, and you believe on yourself hard enough to achieve them. You have a chance to study whatever you want. For example, if you want to be a pilot, you can take few courses and be a pilot. If you want to be a nurse, accountant, or coach, you can study it and become who you want to be. Just pay for your course. If you want to be successful in any area, you can just pay for any course, and you reach your dreams. There is nothing to prevent you from doing what you want, no limitation to your dreams. Unlike other countries, you need to have a specific qualification, you need to have some specific marks to be able to do what you want, and, the worse bit, you need to know somebody who can assist you to enrol on any specific course.

It just ridiculous; you cannot reach your target due to all of obstacles and limitations. That's why, if you are living in UK, don't miss out this opportunity as this is something that other people are dying for. Every day, we see in news that a lot of illegal immigrant do whatever it costs to get to UK. In some cases, they lose their lives. Why is that? Do you think that if they found what they looking for in their countries, they would come here? No. Do you think if their home country could offer them a decent living, they would bother themselves in coming here or even risk their life to be here? No. They are looking for a better life. They are trying to achieve their dreams. They want to feel alive. That's why, if you been lucky enough and you live in UK, make the most of it; go to school, enrol into courses, take part in seminars and workshops, get the degree that you've being dreaming of, and get the job that you want to. Basically, do your best to realise your dreams as this is the place.

In my case, it was a bit hard to find the right job the first time because I was still new to the country, and I didn't have any records yet. My background is in finance, with a degree in audit and management control, but my first job was in nursery. I took this job to help my husband pay the bills and to have the ability to meet people and practice my English more often. I also did it to spend more time with others and learn from their experiences.

Quality life

"The quality of life is more important than the life itself."

-Alexis Carrel

The standard of living in UK is very high compared to other regions or countries. This is not just the cost, but the quality of living to fulfil the basic needs like clothes, food, housing, education, health as well as the level at which physical and other needs are satisfied. Anyone living in UK can have a decent meal and drink if they want to. You are going to say, "But there are homeless in UK as well Khadija." Of course, there are; homelessness exists everywhere. However, if anyone is hungry enough for success, they can change their lives to be successful in their field which will allow them to have a decent life. It can provide, at least, a better life than their back home for sure. If you are living in UK and you are going shopping, you clearly see everyone is buying at least one item. It doesn't matter the age, colour, culture, or religion, everyone is buying clothes, shoes, perfumes, or cosmetic products.

This experience isn't universal to other countries, and it shows that the living standard in UK allows citizens to buy what they want when they want. When compared to the salaries available in the UK, other countries pay much less. I have family and friends abroad who have said they find it hard to pay their bills. They find it hard to find a job, especially after the financial crisis. By the time they say this, I'm just comparing their experience with mine in my head. I found that I'm really lucky being here; it allows me to achieve my goals (obviously with the hard work; nothing comes for free). Hence, if you live in UK, you have double the chance than other people. If you live in UK, you have more chances than someone in another country to achieve your dreams. Be productive, do what makes you happy, follow your passion, and follow your dream. UK is the best place where you can say: I exist, I belong, I'm alive.

Islamophobia

If you Google the definition of Islamophobia you'll find the following:

Islamophobia is the fear, hatred of, or prejudice against the Islamic religion or Muslims generally, especially when seen as a geopolitical force or the source of terrorism. The meaning of the term continues to be debated, and some view it as problematic.

1- 9/11 Incident

The September 11th attacks (also referred to as 9/11) were a series of four coordinated terrorist attacks by the Islamic terrorist group al-Qaeda against the United States that occurred on the morning of Tuesday, September 11, 2001. After this incident, the image of Muslim has completely changed in the world. I was still in Morocco at that time, so it wasn't affecting me directly like others living overseas. It was affecting the economy of our country and, I believe, other Muslim countries as well. I remember the news talking about that the number of tourists decreased due to US's incident and that many hotels and related businesses were affected by the last-minute holiday's cancellations. When my relatives came back to Morocco for holiday in summertime, they used to talk about drawbacks that this incident had on their lives. They were talking about the way they been treated overseas by different people in different places, and how their children were treated in school or universities, how they suffered on the daily basis. It's not fair at all; like the French proverb says: "Payer les pots casses". This means accept responsibility for somebody's fault. In my case, when I moved to UK, I had numerous incidents where I noticed the way people were looking at me or treating me. This is not unique to me; every Muslim person living abroad, especially women wearing the scarf (Hijab), experienced some form of persecution. Other Muslim women who choose to not wear scarf have no issue during their day to day life, at least when compared to us that do. Every day, I felt upset whenever an issue happened. I shared my experience with my husband. He tried to explain the reason behind their behaviour, that I shouldn't take it personally because it's not my fault. He encouraged me to prove that not all Muslims are the same. As I keep saying, in each country, culture, and religion, there is good people and bad people. I'm not talking about everyone here because there are lot of supportive and superb people out there. I'm just talking about a minority who were brainwashed and couldn't make their own judgements.

As a reader of my book, don't let other's judgement affect your decision. As a reader of my book, don't take it personally; you will never change other's assumption on you. As a reader of my book, try to make a difference and prove to the rest of the world that they are wrong. Be the angel who is spreading peace with your surroundings, family, friends, and colleagues. This is the best way to help changing the world's view about Muslim women.

9/11 Consequences

"Wisdom consists of the anticipation of consequences."

-Norman Cousins

In this chapter, I would like to share a few true stories with you that I experienced during my holidays or business trips to European countries as well as some of my friend's experiences in their daily life. After the 9/11 incident, the world view of Islam has totally changed. This is when the issues and problems started. My friends had a hard time, especially in France and Spain. They couldn't go out for a while due to the fact people that would bully and assault them. My friends were treated badly at work by their managers and colleagues; they could see the hate in their eyes, especially from the new persons joining the company. It wasn't easy for them to live a normal life; it wasn't easy for them to go for shopping as they chose to opt for the online option during this period. It wasn't easy for them to practice their normal activities with their kids. Others would stare at them and make them feel uncomfortable. It became painful to be around people. The worse bit occurred in universities and schools. Many students bully Muslims. It doesn't matter if they are wearing the scarf or not as long as they're originally Muslim. The hate grows larger every day, and the media is helping its growth. From videos and pictures, some minorities expand the bad image of Muslims around the globe.

I have friends who couldn't find a job in other European countries because they were wearing a Scarf. What does the Scarf have to do with the ability of the person to do her job? It's totally her choice. Like previously mentioned, if you have the choice to wake up in the morning and put on jeans and a t-shirt, a dress, a skirt with a blouse or whatever, it's your choice isn't it? So why can't you understand that a Muslim woman is wearing a Scarf by choice? Why do most people think this is an obligation by her father, brother, or husband? No, it's not it's a completely an expression on her freedom. Well, my friend couldn't get a job to pay her bills. This was especially true of her rent, and if she doesn't pay it, she will end up in street. She needs to provide food for her six-year-old son who doesn't know what's going on in this world. She just wants to be able to live as others. The sad part of her story was that she ended up being so weak that she accepted her reality and took off her Scarf to please a society that doesn't respect her religion, a society that doesn't respect her choice, a society that doesn't respect her right. This was a society that pretended to be society of freedom but came with exceptions; freedom for some, not all. In tears, she is being forced to take it off to be able to find a job, to be able to feed her family, and to be able to survive. I see this as terrorism in a modern way. It's not just my friend who is being forced to take off her Scarf to be able to survive; I'm sure that there are lot of other women out there who are in the same situation or are still experiencing the same problem. The only choice they have is to give up and change their lives to please others.

Blames and Shames

"Shame and Blame should have no place in our body, mind or spirit."

-Asa Don Brown-

In this part, I will explain the two main struggles that we, as Muslim women, went through or are still going through after the 9/11 incident. You can't imagine the quantity of blame we got and still get from different people belonging to different cultures. As I keep saying, I'm not generalizing. In my book, my experiences were with a few people that I consider minorities that lack any idea about our identity as Muslims or Islam as a religion in general. I remember my experience in Poland; it was very interesting as I previously had few interactions with Polish people in UK. All was confirmed when I went to Poland in business trip to meet up other partner in our office over there. Once I landed in

Warsaw airport, I went to customer service and my adventure began. They kept questioning me. Why am I here? Do I have the names of the people I'm visiting in Warsaw? Do I have a letter from my company, confirming that they are sending me on this business trip? How long am I staying here? Where am I originally from? A ridiculous amount of questions that I never heard before in any of other countries. I travel frequently to different places, but what happened here is just a surprising exception. After leaving the airport, I went to the hotel that I booked and was questioned all over again. Why am I here? What is the name of the company? All sorts of questions. I told them that they are not entitled to ask me these questions. I'm not in police station, and the rest of the hotel's guests haven't gone through the same interrogation.

I was very firm with them, because I saw the way they treated other customers, and the way they were treating me was different. Why? Because I'm wearing the Scarf. I'm paying for the room like their other clients. I'm paying my food and drinks, so they must show some manners, which obviously they don't have. I started to change my tone with them because they confused my niceness with fear.

I'm nice because I'm nice not because I'm scared of the way you going to talk to me or treat me! Guess what? It works. They just changed their behaviour and started showing the customer service they should have had in the first place. The same thing applies to you; yes you, the Muslim woman reading my book now; don't let others treat you in a nasty way. Don't feel humiliated or embarrassed because you are wearing your scarf or that you come from another culture with a different religion. This is your choice; be proud of it. You, the women who are being bullied and mentally abused, it's time to stop hiding behind the blames. It's time to show the world that you deserve to be treated better, to be treated in a good and fair way. You, the reader of my book, you are the one that can help change the way the world treats Muslim women by raising awareness within your family, relatives, friends, colleagues, and the rest of your surroundings.

Mainstream Media

"The mainstream media has its own agenda. They do not want to print the facts. They have an agenda, they have a slant, they have a bias. It is outrageous to me."

-Curt Weldon

In my opinion, the mainstream media affected the Muslim community all over the world by seizing the opportunity to add fuel to the fire. This has a huge impact in our day to day life overseas. Whenever someone sees a Muslim man or woman, they look at us like we are dangerous because of what happened in US. They don't think about how their reaction is hurting us, how their looks are affecting us and our day to day life. This is especially true for Muslim women; we are more likely to get hurt and abused than men. Because of the Hijab we wear, it's clear we are Muslim.

I remember whenever I go with my husband to an event or party, I can see people's reaction like, "What she is doing here? How does she dare to take part of the party? She doesn't drink, so why she is here?" Lot of question mark in their faces and expressing it sometimes by their look. It used to upset me, but I managed to go over it like previously said and now I'm enjoying it to be honest. Whenever I go somewhere and start seeing the funny faces, I just feel more powerful. I feel I am dominating the place and feel like I'm a very famous person with all eyes on me. I just choose to not care anymore about people's behaviour. I don't blame them anymore. I do blame the media who is drawing a wrong image about Muslims all over the world. It's up to me and you to change it and show the rest of the world what Islam is and how can we all live in peace without blaming each other, without judging each other, and without minimizing each other.

It's easy to get caught in the media game, especially if you have no idea about Islam or a Muslim's life. The media doesn't show the good stories about Muslim countries like Malesia, UAE, Bahrein, and Morocco. I would strongly recommend people to research and learn about Islam and Muslim culture, to visit Islamic countries, and approach their Muslim neighbours with questions. This is the only way to make your own judgement; don't be brainwashed by other's opinion. Don't let yourself be a victim of the media because it's easy to be dragged inside this game. By the time you finish this book, I'd hope that you change your mind on the way you look at others, especially if you are quickly influenced by the media. Be the one that brings the changes to life, the one who is making the difference in others life. You never know who needs your help, your support, or your advise. I have seen women who just need someone to listen to them while they talk about their experiences or how they are dealing with the day to day stress overseas. It's never too late to take an action as long as you take it now.

Muslims Seen as the Centre of Attention

As you all know, the Islamophobia myth has expanded very widely after the 9/11 incident, and all eyes are now on Muslim community. The posts in social media are all about what a Muslim has done, how we should stop wearing scarf in public area, and how to not let Muslims work in big companies. There is all sorts of negativity and hate across the web. Other media is a big influencer, looking for to point fingers at a Muslim woman or man who made a tiny mistake. Some seek fake news about Muslim countries or communities to be able to make money and create more conflicts between people. I have friends across Europe that both wear the Scarf and don't that are still suffering from what happened ages ago. Why? Because what has deliberately been created after the incident helped many make other's life hell by spreading hate between all cultures. My friend (J) lost her job because she was banned from wearing her Scarf inside the company in France (which, they said, was supposed to be an open culture). No one helped her or said it's illegal to treat your employees like this. The employer's decision has been approved and supported by HR, and she was sacked for wearing a scarf. How do you see this? What can you say about this situation? I leave it to you to make your own judgement as you might be having the same situation, or a member of your family or friend had it or is still experiencing it. It's not easy to stand out in a culture where you can see few people don't like you because of the culture or religion you came from. How can you decide to like or dislike a person before you approach him or her? It's unfair, and, in my viewpoint, it's just not right.

In my case, it was uncomfortable for me to sit in a coffee shop by myself in the beginning due to the amount of people staring. They made me feel like I shouldn't be there or how on the earth could I dare to think to go for a coffee? It's totally crazy, but it's true. If you're not a Muslim, especially not a Muslim woman with a Scarf, you won't notice what I'm saying or feel what I'm talking about as it doesn't hurt you or affect you directly. However, if you have a family member, friend, or colleague that has experienced it, I'm sure they might share with you their concerns if they were brave enough to talk about it. As previously discussed, people are still too shy to talk about it as they feel like no one can understand what they are talking about or no one can provide them with the necessary guidance and support. The above circumstances help on building up fear inside me about the other cultures based on the assumption that they might harm me or my family somehow. This might occur if I don't pay attention while walking in the street, while talking to strangers, or even working with people. This fear has grown after seeing a few videos that went viral on social medias about the amount of attacks that Muslims were facing or verbal abuses that Muslim have had after any incident happened. This makes my life even harder. Because no one has physically or verbally assaulted me, apart from the stares I get daily, many assume this is all in my head. But it only serves to make my fears grow stronger.

Fear

"Fears are nothing than a state of mind."
-Napoleon Hill

"Extreme fear can neither fight or fly."
-William Shakespeare

Fear was like a prison where all my goals and dreams were kept and hidden due to false evidence appearing real. It wasn't easy for me to get myself out from this state of mind. I remember that I reached a point where I started losing hope in myself, my professional experiences, and my knowledge and skills. I started thinking of giving up working and staying at home, stop going out with my husband, family, or friends, limiting my relationships to people that I really know and are close to me, and not trying to expand my network. I started planning on giving up on all my dreams and goals that I all dreamt of since I was young because I was afraid of other's judgement. It might seem stupid to some of you who never had this experience, but it might seem to be a big issue for the ones who faced the same problem or are still facing it. They just don't have the courage to talk about it in public or are trying, to use a phrase:" to hide the sun with their finger" or, in other words, to not be in trouble by expressing their feelings. Those days were very hard for me; everything starts looking dark, and I began shutting down in silence. Thank God for my precious husband, who was and still is beside me, providing me with the right and necessary guidance and support. He was against my decision on giving up work; he wasn't happy with the idea of giving up on my dreams, especially since he knows how much my goals meant to me.

My husband wasn't accepting any of my excuses; I tried to believe I needed to stop progressing in my life in UK. It was a total madness for him. I trust him a lot. Whatever he said to convince me to get back on track, I tried to find an excuse to believe the rubbish in my head. We went on holiday to Turkey and had a very good time enjoying ourselves.

I scrubbed each stupid idea I used to have and replaced it with a fresh and new mindset to be even more hungry for success. I changed my job to something even better where I got promoted in less than a year due to the progress I showed in my work. I started giving motivational speeches to my community and talking about my experience, how I was about to ruin my future and my hunger for success by letting myself believe false ideas. I provided other women, mostly friends, my assistance to overcome their situation and take the lead to progress and improve their life. Don't let yourself be a victim of your thoughts; no enemy is going to harm us more than the enemy inside us. Don't let other's judgement of you become your reality. Defeat the negativity around you, be motivated, and, especially, be yourself.

Judging the Book by the Cover

"Judging a person don't define who they are; it defines who you are."

-Unknown

Staring

After the 9/11 incident, I would say that it's getting hard for me to live my normal life as I want to. When I'm going shopping, people sometimes looking at me like I have two heads, like I'm not supposed to go out. It feels to me like I'm not allowed to do basic things in my life. When I went on holiday, this was where I noticed it the most. It was 2015, and my first holiday to a European country after I came to England. My husband and I went to Malta in August. It's a very lovely place; warm weather, the beaches are just amazing, and the water is wonderful. I loved it. The sad part of this is that I spent two weeks crying every day. The way people looked at me transformed my holiday into hell. I can see people looking at me when I go for breakfast in the hotel, while I'm in pool playing with my stepson, or while I'm on the beach. It was so annoying that I told my husband that I could not stay in this horrible place anymore. The holiday where we supposed to laugh, enjoy our life, and forgot about any stress just turned out to a be nightmare. My husband starts getting stressed too in the beginning, and whenever someone is looking at me, he tells them off and swears at them. He argues and debates with people about Islam. It was heart breaking for him to see me in such a state, getting destroyed by people's judgement. I remember when we went outside for lunch or dinner in a restaurant, people keep looking at me from time to time like I'm a weird creature. It's annoying as I'm not enjoying the moment with my husband or friends anymore. I started doubting myself like something was wrong with me. Am I ugly to the point that I'm grabbing people's attention? Am I scary to a point that everyone is looking at me? I don't know what they think, to be honest, because I cannot read their mind; however, I know how it felt for me. It's a very nasty feeling. I don't feel comfortable at all. I feel that I need to watch how I'm talking, walking, and reacting.

I feel like I need to pay extra attention, so I won't miss something. I don't feel like myself. I start feeling like I'm pretending to be someone else, which has a big effect on my mental health. I don't feel comfortable, even at home, especially because I have been out all day working and spent more than seven hours trying to please others, which took too much for my mental energy. Basically, I started losing myself by being trapped in this rat race. I know you might be in the same situation and you are probably still suffering from it or are still trying to recover from it right now. My only advise is that if you don't help yourself to come out from this trap, nobody can. You need to believe in yourself first so others can provide you with the necessary assistance and guidance. Keeping quiet and not talking about it will just accumulate the issue inside you and affect your mental health in a way that might destroy your life. You are human as well, and you deserve to be treated fairly and with total respect.

Work Ethic

One of the places where I do see people's judgement is at work. We all know that UK is a very multicultural country. In my previous workplaces, most of my colleagues are originally from different countries, like East and West Europe and North and South America. Sometimes, they bring cakes, and they just split it between them without asking me if I want some or not. They buy presents for each other's birthdays or whenever they come back from a holiday, and I never felt included. It was very hard for me to work in such an environment, especially since I came from a culture where sharing and caring means everything. When I was in my second job, I used to have an Eastern European colleague who has no qualifications in finance but still pretending that she knew it all. When she talks, it's clear that everything she says is just about herself. There is no teamwork at all in her language. She likes being bossy and controlling others. Hence, she tried to do the same with me. She did this because she thinks I don't know what I'm doing, especially because I don't praise my work as I should. This was one of my mistakes, not praising myself enough front of management. It was so embarrassing in a meeting when people don't give me chance to talk about my opinion or share any good ideas. I sometimes feel they don't ask me because they think the Scarf, which is covering my head, is covering my mind and thoughts too. This is not true. Muslim women are like any other women. The only difference is we cover our hair by choice. I would always come home, crying and whining to my husband, who was very frustrated about the situation. He was my biggest support as always and still is in all situations. He was the one who was teaching me how to control my feelings. He made me ask myself questions like: How do I stop others from minimizing me at work? How do I become patient in situations and not cry in front people as this will show how fragile I am? However, from my side, I took literally every word he said, every piece of advice, and I applied it accordingly. And guess what; it works. I stood up for myself at work and stopped my colleague from treating me badly as she used to. I stopped anybody else moving forwards who wants to put me down in front of my family, friends, and colleagues and any person who wanted to make me feel bad just because I'm wearing a Scarf. I learned how to defend myself in a shitty situation. I learned how to take charge and talk about projects, ideas, and solutions. I learned to be powerful.

Marginalisation vs Integration

This mostly happens at work more than any other place. Whenever I started a job, I'm not everyone's cup of tea, which is normal; I don't expect myself to be anyway. However, we still need to have some manners and respect towards others. There are times where my colleagues get together and invite each other for tea and coffee, and no one asks me if I want something. I feel really left out. It used to hurt me so much. I would get back home after work and speak to my husband about it. My husband's advise was always useful. He advised me to not take it personal, as they probably don't know me yet. Try to offer them coffee or tea instead or try to get them some cakes or sweets from time to time. They get used to you offering rather than receiving, and then they will start offering you too. I tried it, and it worked. Whatever he said or thought was correct. So, I started offering my colleague teas and coffees. The first time, no one wanted to have anything. The second time was the same, but third time, one of them said yes (third time's the lucky charm).

I made it for her, and she thanked me. The next time I offered, two of my colleagues said, "Let's go!" The three of us went to the kitchen and started chatting about our plans for holiday, talking about Morocco, and how amazed they were by the Moroccan food (they been previously to Marrakech and Tangier). It was a starting point to know each other more. I started baking as I like baking during weekends, so I made Baklava (a Syrian sweet with filo pastry, pistachios, and almonds soaked in honey). I took it with me on Monday morning. At 10 am, I put it on my desk and told all of my colleagues to help themselves. I offered coffee and tea, and, this time, four people said yes. I went to the kitchen to make the drinks; when I came back, the whole department was by my desk. I was hugely surprised. "What's going on?" They were all fascinated by the flavour of the sweet, and everyone was asking me about the recipe. I was very happy that day as I wasn't expecting that small gesture could make such a huge difference in my life.

From that day on, most people kept coming to me, sharing their experiences of trying to make Baklava. Some were very successful and some not. We chat about it, and I gave them tips on how to

Judging the Book by the Cover

make it properly. It was such a simple and amazing discussion, which made me very pleased. The lesson learned from this experience is that don't wait for people to accept you, don't wait for people to read your mind or feel what you're feeling. You need to take ownership of your situation. Your need to approach them in a nice way. Show them who you are, how nice you are, and How much you care? Do some gestures for them, and I'm sure they will appreciate it? Don't judge them or blame them; be the one who takes the initiative and turn on the light in dark moments. Things like this happen everywhere and with anyone not just because you are Muslim. Some people need more time than others to accept new persons. Give them a chance to find their own way to approach you. Be understanding and take the lead to make things happen and bring the changes to life.

Low Self-esteem

"Low self-esteem involves imagining the worst that other people can think about you."
-Roger Elbert

Going through most of the things that I listed above, I started losing confidence in myself. I started doubting myself in minor things, which I never did before. For example, I noticed that if I went shopping and someone dropped a packet of crisp from the shelf, I say sorry even though it's not me who dropped it. Or when I'm queuing waiting for my coffee to be served in Starbucks and the person behind me jumped the queue, I say sorry. It's ridiculous. It's not even my fault, and I'm saying sorry. Sorry for what? I cannot believe it when I remember it. This is all related to a lack of confidence, I started losing my self-esteem I started feeling that everything is my fault even its not. My normal life became complicated for no reason because I started believing others' opinions, which is wrong. Les Brown said, "Don't let somebody's opinion be your reality." I totally agree; I experienced it myself. I believed in others' judgement of me. I believed in others' opinions, which led to me beginning to lose my confidence and myself. It's not easy to fight this situation, especially if you were by yourself and have no one to speak to. Luckily, I have my husband beside me. It will take from your dreams, take from your time, take from your feeling, and, most importantly, this fear will take from your life. That's why you need to do something about it. If it's not easy for you, at least try to do something about it to see the difference. The world is not bad at all. In every country, every religion, every culture there are good people and bad people. Be proud of yourself whenever you are one of the good ones. If you are reading this book and you are experiencing the same thing in silence, it's time to come out of your shell and speak up.

If you are reading this book and you are living the same thing, it's time to make the change for your life and talk about your feeling or ask for help from your family, relatives, or friends. If you are reading this book and you know someone who might need your help, please offer your help even they never talk to you about it. If you read this book and you know that you can make changes for people around you, please take the initiative and do it. There is much to do, because I know many people from different cultures who are really amazing and tolerant and can do their best to support and assist others. It doesn't matter to them what your gender, your colour, your religion, or your culture is. They are angels on the earth, feeling an overwhelming need to help someone else. We really need to see more of these kind of people nowadays. With all the bad news, hate, and wars currently going on, we need Angles on earth to help us change our thoughts and our behaviours towards others to be able to live in peace.

Judgement Clouds the Mind

"Be Curious, not Judgmental."

-Walt Whitman

When you decide to move to a new country where you have no family, relatives, or friends, it is hard to quickly integrate, especially if it's not similar to your culture. In my case, moving to UK was a big change in my life, because I left all my family and friends behind to be with love of my life. I can say it was worth it even though wasn't easy. First, I grew up in a warm nice place in Morocco named Agadir. If you have never been or heard about it, I would advise you to do visit; it's sunny mostly all year around, with nice weather, lovely beaches, golden sand, and delicious food. It's marvellous. Once I moved here, it was a 180-degree change for me; it was a new culture, different people, different weather, and different language, especially since I speak just

French and Arabic. However, I liked the weather for some reason. You going to say I'm mad. Well, I'm not, no, but I probably had enough from hot weather in Morocco, and England was heaven for me. I struggled the first time to understand what people were saying; in Morocco, they teach us formal American, which we use in high schools, universities, and business, so understanding English people was a challenge. I remember when I got my first job, there was a great mixture of people, English, Polish, Pakistani, Italian, Indian, Mexican, French, and so on. During our team meeting, we were discussing issues that we are facing and trying to find a solution for it. Whenever I came up with an idea, some colleagues didn't like it or tried to be against it for some reason. Thank God for my manager who was a fair person as she doesn't judge by the look, colour, gender, or race. If something is correct and can solve the issue, she is praising it and makes sure that she provided me with the necessary credit.

This caused me problems with them because they treated me differently. They didn't invite me during lunch break or when they go out for drinks. I discussed it with my manager who was very understanding

Judgement Clouds the Mind

and advised to not take it personally. Few people find it very hard to accept others from different cultures. Her advice still serves me now. Whenever I started to take their behaviours personally, I remember her magical advice and switch my mind from the negativity to positivity. It wasn't an easy change for me to keep switching my mindset throughout these cases; however, it all depends on you and how you would like to change your life. I worked very hard on myself to be in the place where I am now, and I thank God and my husband for his support all this time and for his assistance and advise, which are priceless. If you are still suffering from the societal judgement and you think you need support to overcome the situation where you are now, don't hesitate to reach out to me for advise. I'll provide you with the necessary support, and why not be part of the inspirational community so you can help others as well? Everything is possible if you believe in yourself, you have a willingness to challenge your circumstances, and work to make a difference in the world. The world needs people who are willing to serve the humanity without any price, people who can deliver their best to make up a better life for others. Be the one and start from today as its never late.

Discrimination/Depression

"No one is born hating another person because of the colour of his skin or his background or his religion. People must learn to hate and if they can learn to hate they can be taught to love, for love comes more naturally to the human heart than its opposite."

-Nelson Mandela

As per the above quote from the great men Nelson Mandela, no one is born with hate. It's all learned from our environment or taught by our parent, family, friends, or strangers in our life. In this case, why are we spreading it through our kids who don't know anything, especially about news, religions, or cultures? It's so heart-warming when I see kids from different cultures, skin colours, or gender playing football together, swinging, or other games without noticing any differences between them. However, all these prejudices start building up as they grow, and I'm blaming the parents who teach their kids the wrong message and wrong attitude toward other cultures. Just because the parents had a previous bad experience with one person doesn't give you the right to teach your kids wrongly. While writing about this topic, I remembered incidents that I experienced myself while travelling across Europe as well as UK; they're unforgettable. Living with the feeling of non-belonging is not easy, especially if all the external factors (at work, university, shops, parks and so on) confirm it. This feeling makes me wonder if my decision to move to UK was a right decision in the first place. I started doubting myself and my ability to make decisions about my personal life. Having said that, it reminds me of a friend living in France who was still suffering from depression due to the way she was being treated, the way she was being seen, and the way she was being abused by others. She struggled to find her path to become herself, she lost faith in her personality. She lost faith in her ability to cope with the people around her, even the close ones: family and friends.

I didn't want to follow the same route and end up in the same situation, living with insecurity, self-doubt, and depression as this will affect my career, my personal life, and me as a person. Just thinking of it makes me feel sick. That's why I challenged the situation, environment, people, and, especially, I challenged myself and my thoughts because this is the most destroying factor. Many times, we don't recognise this until we end up in a situation where it's hard to stand up again and face the life. Many women are still suffering in silence and choose to keep quiet, even refusing to open up to the person closest to them. However, from this book I want you, yes, I'm talking to you, to get up from where you are and face a mirror and say the following:

"I'm strong. I'm not afraid of anything. I believe on myself. I believe in my ability to be the person that I want to. I can do it. I'm going to do it, and no one can stop me from reaching my goals."

Say it from your heart and believe it. Say it every day. Say it whenever you feel you need some push or a kick to motivate yourself, and I'm sure you can do it.

The Importance of Having Support

"Through Thick or Thin, I'll accept you at your strongest yet Love and support you at your weakest."

-Pure Love Quote

Family Support

"To us, family means putting your arms around each other and being there."

-Barbara Bush

Support is very essential for every woman living overseas. This is important if it is coming from her very close family like her husband, parents, brother, or sisters. In my case, my husband played a fundamental role in my entire life. He has been very supportive through my whole journey, and he is still supporting me on any idea, thought, and project I come up with. During holiday time, where most of the times we going to Malta, Italy, or Spain, I ended up in a stressful situation due to people's judgement. I almost made myself believe that I'm not allowed to have holiday with my family, like I'm not human being who is working very hard to deserve some stress-free time. My husband was the one who was trying to make me feel more comfortable, trying to make me happier, and do whatever It takes for him to make me cheerful. His main focus was to prevent me from being upset. trying his best to shift my attention from thinking of other's perception to focus on the weather, beach, food, and enjoy the moment together. I'll never forget my first experience in Malta, where I was really upset and crying every day because people keep looking at me whenever I go: in hotel's lounge, pool, restaurant, gym by the sea, in market, in a boat, literally everywhere. However, my husband, or, I should say, my angel, was always there to protect, entertain, support, assist, and love me. I do owe him too much for what he has done for me through this hard time. I would strongly advise you as a parent, family, friends, or stranger, to be the one who is supporting and willing to give assistance whenever is needed. You never know; you might be the angel of someone who lost hope, the motivator for someone who lost interest, the guardian for someone who needs to feel secure. You, as a reader of my book, be the messenger who's spreading peace around you. Changes start from inside.

Role of Friends

"A friend is one who overlooks your broken fence and admires the flowers in your garden."

-GH

Having friends from the same cultures sometimes doesn't help you to go over the situation that you are facing daily. They might make your worse by whining all the time. However, having friends from different cultures is the best way to overcome your situation, because this gives you the feeling that other cultures accept you, that other cultures have no problem with your religion, that other cultures do understand your point when you talk about your situation as they might face the same thing but differently. I do remember when I was working my 2nd job in UK, I have different friends from different countries:

Netherlands, Mexico, Germany, France, Italy, Turkey, and South Africa, and so on. They are so amazing, and we still keep in touch, even though we're not working together like we used to be. We still get together once every so often to have a meal together and talk about all the good memories and how much fun we had together. We spoke about our experience of being foreigners in UK and how much it affects us sometimes when people look at us strangely or oddly. It brings up questions like: Are we not human like the others? Are we not allowed to live all together? Well, we all know the answer is yes. However, some closed minds ignore the fact that we all the same, no one is better than the other, no one is higher than the other, and no one is more important than the other. I remember one Mexican friend was working as a credit controller in a big company. She was paid less than the other controllers even though she speaks more languages than others just because she wasn't our line manager's favourite. He refused to give her any pay raise or bonus without any reason and without any justification. She discussed the issue with the HR department who conducted a huge investigation about the issue where the supervisor and the manager were both involved. It wasn't easy for her to stay working while being in HR meetings in front of her supervisor (which makes her life even worse). By end of the day, the supervisor was suspended because of the unfair treatment of this woman. The Mexican lady finally received the pay raise that she dreamt of, and now she is supporting all other women with the same issue.

I would say to each woman who is facing the same issue or having the same problem in her work that you need to raise the problem directly and fairly with the company's HR. They will provide you with the necessary assistance. I wouldn't advise any woman who is reading my book to keep silent about any abusive situation, at home, outside, at work, or school. However, as long as you talk about it, discuss it, and share your experience with others a few wonderful things will happen. First, you start feeling better because you will realise that you are not the only one living in the same situation. Second, you will be helping other women talk and express themselves, especially the ones who are suffering in silence and don't feel comfortable speaking to strangers. You will help build their confidence and give them the power needed to seek help, ask for assistance, and contact the right person for support.

Nobody has the right to treat you in an unfair way in your workplace or treat you like you don't have or add any value to what you doing. We all have the capacity and capability to deliver the best of us.

Colleagues

"Good colleagues are those who know that WE is more than ME."

-WM.com

Each one of us spend more time at work than with our family and friends. Means, being supported by your colleagues is essential to be successful at work. However , in my case, it was very difficult to make colleagues that can support me through this journey or provide me with any guidance because I used to be a shy, very closed person, honestly scared of what others can say about me as Muslim woman and that fact that English was my third language. It was very hard for me to challenge myself and fight my thoughts and go sit with my colleagues at lunch time. I used to work during my lunch time just to avoid sitting with people, just to avoid any annoying questions about my religion, and any annoying questions about my background. Why? It was because fear was controlling me. Not being surrounded with the right people contributes a lot on keeping yourself controvert. This helps your negative thoughts to grow, dominate, and control your mind. I'm lucky that I had a very supportive manager who believed in my hard work, who believed in my opinion, who believed in my ideas, and encouraged me to speak up, to talk freely about anything I believe is true and feel confident about it. I know you might have had the same problem as me, or you might still be having the same issue as me. I would strongly suggest you come out from your shell and free yourself from these false thoughts, to believe in yourself, speak up, and stand up for your rights. Do you know why? Because if you don't do it, nobody can do it for you. You are in charge of your life; you are the artist of your life, you are the one who decides the picture that you want to draw, either a clear blue sky or a dark night. You have the choice.

It's important to have the support of your workmates as this is the place where you spend most of your time as previously said. That's why having support from your line manager, someone in your team, or somebody from another department is essential. Previously, I spent my lunch break just working, trying to avoid sitting with others. I didn't know if they wanted me sitting with them or if I'm make them feel obligated to sit with me, which is even worse. However, it was all in my mind. After a few weeks, they noticed that I'm not sitting with them, and they start offering to join them, which I did, and I'm glad I did it instead of refusing. Our relationship has dramatically improved since that time. Sometimes, our imagination brings some weird thoughts that doesn't actually exist. If you work, get involved within your colleagues, have lunch with them, go for drinks after work just to network more with them, offer teas and coffees, care about them, and you will notice the difference in your workplace and life. Be open to all, respect all, and care about others. Colleagues are the second family in your life, and it's always good to feel you belong to this family.

Schools and Organisations

The most important thing that I would strongly advise the parent to do is support their kids and work on building their confidence, especially if you have a young girl, wearing her Hijab, and she is still at school or just graduated or in process of looking for a job. It doesn't matter which stage she is in; she will definitely need your support. Your daughter, sister, or wife will need your ongoing assistance to stand up in any situation she is going to face. There might be kids at school calling her names because she is wearing hijab, and she never told you about it just to not make it worse, or she is probably being scared at having more trouble at school. She might be keeping it to herself, which can lead to depression. Communication is the main key in this situation. Try to communicate every day with your daughter, sister, or wife. Ask her how her day was at school, at work, or outside the house. Be the supportive, father, brother, or husband; take the lead and assist. I know many women who would die for someone to ask them about themselves and their feelings. Ask them how they survive during the hard times. They need your support, they need your help, and they need your assistance. By offering all of the above, I'm sure they going to feel more comfortable, more confident about themselves, and more powerful as they know that someone has their back and that there is nothing to be afraid of. As a reader of my book, don't be one of the silent people. Ask for help whenever it is needed. Don't wait for people to read your mind, don't wait for others to feel what you feel, to be in your shoes. Ask for their assistance, ask for their support, and ask for their feedback. I'm sure people cannot turn their back on you if you need them. It doesn't make sense to keep quiet and suffer in silence. This is not going to help you go over your situation; it's just going to make it worse, especially if you have kids. This will affect them indirectly when they see you crying whenever you get abused in shops, parks, restaurants, and so on. Kids understand a lot of what is going on without talking or expressing it. That's why it will be good to communicate your feelings instead of continuing to cry in such situations or hide it inside. Try to communicate, to stand up for yourself. As I keep saying, no one has the right to treat you badly. We are all human, and we all deserve to live in peace.

Build up a strong personality that can serve you in many situations at school, universities, and work. Help yourself first before asking someone else for help. You know yourself better than anybody else, so you know exactly what you need to be stronger and more courageous, enough to stand up for yourself. Then figure out how to overcome your situation by listening the online videos, taking part in online groups, and so on. I'm sure there are many organisations and online groups that offer free help. You are responsible for your life, so live it in the way you want, not the way others want. Don't ever feel humiliated or shy. Be proud of your origins, proud of your culture, and proud of your religion wherever you go.

Media

"Whoever controls the media, controls the mind."

-Jim Morrison

Social media plays a huge role on the way others see Muslims, especially Muslim women, in Western society. Most people think that each woman who is wearing a Scarf is forced to wear it; which is completely rubbish. We live in a modern society now, and freedom is essential in each culture. Women is Islam have their freedom and wearing the Scarf is a choice. Some women choose to wear it, and some choose not to. If I choose to wear it, it's because it's my choice of what I feel comfortable with more than anything else. I believe my choice should be respected as well. Just imagine: you wake up in the morning and put on your suit, your dress, shorts and a T-shirt, or skirt before you go out. That's your choice isn't it? Nobody asked you to wear a specific set, and no one can do it because you have the ability to choose what to wear. It's called freedom, and the same thing goes for me or any women in similar case. I woke up in the morning, and I have a wardrobe full of scarves with different colours and shapes that I like to choose from and take the one that suits my outfit. You know, sometimes, there are certain types of people who have collections of watches, collections of ties, and jewels. In my case, it's scarves. I like to have different colours and different sorts of materials (warm for winter and light for summer). I like to check magazines for different Muslim models with new outfit collections so I can order from them. You might have probably noticed that recently there are many companies modelling Islamic outfits with a modern twist, which make it even cool.

Unfortunately, we don't see that in the media nowadays in Western society. This would be how people could see who we are and how we live. That's why I don't blame anyone; this is not their fault, especially if they never had the chance to visit a Muslim country like Morocco, Tunisia, or the Middle East. Where else could they see a huge difference from what they have heard about us in media and what is reality? If they did, they could distinguish the truth from the lies. As a Muslim woman reading my book, try to post a positive word, sentence, or picture on your social media to share positivity with others. As a reader of my book who has been a victim of the media and who has started to see things differently or is starting to discover the truth about Islam, share your thoughts on social media. This is priceless.

Muslim Community

Living in an area where you have neighbours or friends from the same community plays an important role in getting over the depression and anxiety that is sometimes related to this issue. At least you can find someone who has been through the same issue and who might be helpful to you and provide you with the necessary support and guidance. You might find help in someone who has a different point of view than yours. I can see groups in Facebook where other communities help, assist, and support each other by organising a lunch for everyone in a restaurant or park. Go for a trip to some interesting places where you can all spend

Media

time together as well as organise some event where they can represent their culture to others. This is very interesting mainly for the new arrivals in UK. In my case, I wasn't lucky enough to have someone close to me (I mean a Moroccan community), however, I tried to have more connexion with other people from other countries as it's good to have a variety of friends representing different cultures where you will have a chance to learn from them while studying, working, or having your own business. I recommend any Muslim women who is living in UK or any other European country to get involved within her community as much as possible. This will help build her confidence in terms of language by meeting new people each time and practicing it comfortably when talking to others.

After spending more time with people in your community, this will help you to build long term relationships with them, and you are going to be able to invite them to your house to share your culture with them or by cooking different foods during any events held in your community centre. This is the best and easiest way to give them an idea about your origins and background. I do believe keeping in touch with your community helps you to come out from your comfort zone to discover the outside world, which is very important to you and your family while you are living abroad. You cannot stay indoors for your whole life; it's impossible, especially if you have kids. You have to take them to school, parks, etc. It's not just about you; it's about your family too. Don't be afraid of asking others to join them. Don't be scared of people's reactions. Don't get offended from people's rejection. This will happen anyway somehow. You need to focus on what you really want in life, how you want to progress, and what will make you achieve your goals. Failures are a part of life; there is no way to get rid of them. We need to be more responsible and think wisely about how we can transform failure to a success. There are many books on the market teaching self-development and how to succeed in your life. Take the initiative and read and read and read until you learn and keep practicing until you achieve your goals. Nothing is easy, but everything is possible in life if we work hard enough to reach it.

Importance of Integration

"A democracy depends on the full integration of women into society, especially on seeing to it that they have equal access to the same tools of opportunity as men."

-Hilary Clinton

In this chapter, I will go though few steps which might be helpful in overcoming your situation. It doesn't matter how bad it is, every situation is solvable. Just read my tips, focus, and follow my tips. What I'm going to walk you through is how to build your self-confidence while you are living in an overseas country. This is a guide to follow if you are interested in getting involved in your new society, which will boost your feeling of belonging. Nobody on earth is born with self-esteem. If you see someone that has incredible self-confidence, it's not because they are born with it. It's because he or she has worked on improving themselves for years. The same thing applies to you. You need to work continuously on yourself if you want to be stronger. My step by step guide is simple and was very useful. It helped me become who I am today and helped me to overcome all the situations and problems I previously faced at work, on holidays, in shopping centres, parks, and many different places. It is still helping me with any new challenges I'm facing in my daily life. What I'm discussing in my book has never stopped and will never stop unless the people's mentality changes. This will be difficult, if even possible, especially with all the crazy things happening in the world.

If you are still finding it difficult to get involved and become integrated within the society, it's probably not because of the external factors. It might be just your thoughts holding you back from progressing and achieving your goals or your worries stopping you from moving forwards and taking the initiative to overcome your fears. Be the person that you want to be. Don't let yourself get stuck in the rat race. You will never overcome your excuses or fears because of yourself. Yes, you. It's easy to notice if somebody is holding you back or stopping you from achieving your goals. It's easy to catch those persons, but it's hard to notice ourselves when we give ourselves excuses. It's hard to stop our thoughts from destroying our dreams. It's hard to control our minds when they have no desire to succeed anymore. Your worst enemy is you unless you work nonstop on yourself.

Learn the Language

"Language is to the mind more than light is to the eye."

-William Gibson

"Knowledge of language is the doorway to wisdom."

-Roger Bacon

The key element to success in a foreign country is the language. You need to learn the language to be able to interact within the society. Without language, you cannot progress in your life, and you won't be able to even get yourself something to eat or drink. We should be frank with ourselves. Studying the language opens the door for many opportunities, allows you to interact with people and get involved in the society freely without any issues. Before moving to UK, English was a part of my studies as well as French. We have been taught American English more than British English in Morocco, but it was still helpful for me once I moved to UK. At least I was able to communicate with people wherever I go. I was able to go out and buy myself things I needed like clothes, food, etc. I was able to sit in a coffee shop and order my coffee and a muffin. Ordering coffee in a coffee shop seems very simple; however, it's a huge step for me due to the big difference between UK and Morocco or UK and other European countries. Whenever I meet any women who have just moved to UK, coming from East Europe, Middle East, or North Africa. My main advice to her is to learn the language first and don't rely on her family or friends or anybody else. They have their own lives, responsibilities, and they cannot be with you every day.

There are many ways to learn English, French, German, Italian or any other language depending on where you live. Sign up for group chat in WhatsApp or Facebook to meet other people sharing the same purpose; learn from each other. You can watch plenty of YouTube videos, which are very useful and helpful, especially those which explain each step slowly and clearly. You can easily listen to music and watch films on TV; it's a good way to know more about the culture. Last and not least, enrol into classes within your community where you can meet people face to face and learn from a teacher who will provide you with any support or assistance needed. I believe this is a good way to know more people within the same situation; it's a way to have new friends to hang out with. If you really want to be involved within your new society, you need to take the advantage of the different materials you have. Some don't have a chance to be here and change their life. Don't isolate yourself from the outside life because you feel shy, especially with different people from different cultures. It's a total jerk; it's all in your mind. You need to feel that you belong to this society by learning how to integrate within the culture and by trying to make a difference with a positive impact.

Get Involved within the Community

"The greatness of a community is most accurately measured by the compassionate actions of its members."

-Coretta Scot King

I recommend any Muslim women who lives in UK, especially or any other European country, to get involved within her community as much as possible; this will help with building her confidence in terms of language by meeting new people, practicing her new language, and feeling more comfortable when she is talking to others. You will build confidence by gaining new friendships. This happens when you spend time with the persons in your community day after day; this will help you build a long-term relationship with them, be able to invite them to your house and share with them your culture, and be able to cook different foods during any events held in your community centre. This is the best and easy way to give them an idea about your background and origin. I do believe in keeping in touch with your community. This will help you come out from your comfort zone to discover the outside world. That is very interesting to you and your family. Don't be afraid of asking others in your area to join them whenever there is a charity event or a neighbourhood party to meet and greet each other. Don't be scared of people's reaction. If you approach them, they might just not be used to you as a new member within their community. Don't get offended from people's rejection because this will happen somehow anyway. You need to focus on what you really want in life, how you want to progress, and what will make you achieve your goals. This is what you should worry about, not other's opinion or other's judgement. You cannot control people, but you still can control yourself.

Start from your community to reach out to the whole world. Offer your help and assistance to people who need it. This is a good way to make

Get Involved within the Community 81

yourself well known within people in your area. Years ago, whenever there was a community event, I was the one who made food like the Moroccan cuisine. Couscous and Tajine were always present at these events. This was really a good way to introduce people to Mediterranean cuisine, the kind where you cannot resist the favours it's a finger licking foods. You can start doing the same thing at the beginning to introduce yourself to people. It is a good way to get to know you, your background, and your culture. If you're not confident or comfortable enough to get involved within a big number of people. Start with your neighbours by showing them your culture by sharing foods or cakes. You can buy biscuits from the shop and give it to your next-door neighbour during Christmas or Easter time. Say, "Thank you for being my neighbour", and you will see her reaction. I'm sure they are going to be surprised as they would never expect such gesture from you. Some of you are going to feel like I'm pushing you hard to do something that they are not comfortable with. Believe me; I was the same, but when I started doing it, it made such a big difference. I now feel like I'm live among family instead of neighbours. I'm talking from experience. I've done it many times, and, each time, it proves that it does work. Trust me; if you would like to change your life to be better, start making difference in other's life.

Start Working

"Work is the most important thing in life which distracts from every misfortune."
                                             -Ernest Hemingway

Working is very essential for anyone who just comes to UK or any other oversee country, especially women because this is the best way to feel you're integrating into the country. Don't be like the ones who choose to stay at home and get benefits from the government. This is ridiculous, because they don't know how much they missed from their life. They are relying on benefits that they could get more from working in a decent job. As a new arrival, I would strongly recommend looking for a job that is related to your qualifications. You know what to do and how to do it until you reach the job that you always dream of. The first thing is to obtain all of your qualifications translated to English if you come from a country where English is not the first language. I won't be recommending any organisation in my book, but you should be able to find plenty in the internet with a reasonable price. While waiting for your diplomat and qualifications to be translated, try to build up your CV in a professional way to make it easier for yourself if you want to apply for any job. Just follow instructions you find on Google or YouTube. You will be fine creating one, or you can get a professional person to do it for you. After having your translated documents and CV ready, start contacting the recruiting agencies by phone or email to introduce yourself and show them your interest in looking for a job that suits your qualification and skills.

You will be really surprised about the amounts of emails or calls you are going to receive from different companies to get your first interview. The instructions I'm giving you seem very easy to follow; however, many people struggle to find an organisation to get their certificates translated, because they never thought of it. Sometimes, they just don't have the ability to look and dig in the internet for the useful information. Don't stop at the first obstacle you face in your life; there will be problems all the way through. Keep yourself strong and carry on. Don't take the easy choice and sit at home, just looking after your kids without doing anything that makes you feel alive and contribute to the community and to the country. A percentage of immigrants choose to not work and rely on the country's benefits. This is wrong in my opinion, especially the ones who can work and don't suffer from any disability. Why waste your life getting a small amount of the benefits when you have the chance to progress and improve your life by working in a job that can provide you with a good lifestyle? Having a decent job is very important to getting to know people, meet people, and stay connected with the society. Stay up to date with any changes of the law, the system, or anything happening around you.

Be Inspirational

"Try to be rainbow in someone else's cloud."
                                    -Maya Angelou

Live your life for others, and you will discover another taste and meaning of your existence. Helping is a very powerful message, and it serves as a lesson to people who doesn't expect it from you. Starting with your neighbours, share your food with people who need it or the ones who don't have any one to cook for them. This is especially true for the elderly; they stay at home without kids around or family to visit them. Offer your help to your co-workers by assisting whenever they are stuck on a task or cannot understand a process. Provide your guidance if they have to deliver a project on time. You can still offer coffee or tea if you see they are too busy to make one for themselves. My favourite one is what I'm doing with my friends;

I love inviting them for a meal at home. They love Moroccan food, so I feel very happy and pleased whenever I invite them for a lunch or dinner where I share the best flavoured and tasty Moroccan food. We sit and chat for a couple of hours; sometimes we arrange to meet up outside at a restaurant and spend the afternoon or evening together. It's the small gestures that make difference in people's life. You don't need to spend a lot of money or buy expensive gifts to get them accept you. It's totally wrong. I believe in being nice, being kind, and being helpful whenever it is needed. Listening to people is the most important thing in life. While I'm writing this chapter, I remember an advert on TV where they said 2 million people in UK don't have anyone to talk too, especially the elderly. It broke my heart when I heard a lady saying that, sometimes, she walks to shops so she can meet people and talk to them, because she doesn't have kids and none of her family visits her. You cannot imagine how hard it is for these people to live in these situations. Putting a smile on somebody's face can mean more than giving them money. Live your life by making other's life happy. It's a great symbol of caring. Always remember: "What goes around comes around." It's true. When you make a difference in someone's life, or you helped them to achieve what they want. Help them achieve their dreams. You are going to be fulfilled, and you will try to give even more. As a human being, you feel fulfilled and happy whenever you help and support others.

It always feels good if people can remember you as a person who makes a difference in their life, a person who leaves a positive impact. I always encourage people to be kind to others and share kindness and courteousness with everyone, young or old, black or white, Muslim or other religion. It doesn't matter who you are; what matters is how you treat people and what value you add to them.

Build Mental & Emotional Strength

"My strength did not come from lifting weights. My strength came from lifting myself up when I was knocked down."

-Bob Moore

Working on your mental health is very important during these kind of situations as it allows you to face any challenge or obstacle with an open mind, especially in cases where you were abused by strangers in shops, parks, holidays, or when you are bullied or neglected by your neighbours or colleagues at work. You don't need to be a psychologist to be mentally strong. You need to find a better way to take yourself out from the daily stress. There are many ways on how you remove negative thoughts.

There are many different steps to follow to be stress and anxiety free and many tips and tricks on how to help yourself to overcome any bad situation. You could go to the gym. I used to go to the gym with my husband every day after work and trained for at least one good hour, have a shower, and then back home for dinner. I felt alive. I felt that I wanted to do more, that I wanted to progress more in my life. You feel an immense energy running all over. You know the important thing you feel after exercising, that you have lot of energy for your family, kids, husband, parents, and yourself, most importantly. One of the ways I take release stress is baking. I enjoyed baking cape cakes, Moroccan cakes, and Mediterranean sweets, which I love too much. I used to spend part of my weekends baking something new, learning new cakes from different cuisines, which makes me happy. I enjoy discovering new flavours and eating the cake at the end of the day. Reading is one of my big push to take the decision and start writing my proper book, especially after reading many motivational and inspirational books from well know persons like Les Brown, Marie Forleo, Mel Robins, Michelle Obama, and so on. It is very important to find your resting point. This means that the thing you do to feel relaxed and help release dopamine, to feel happy and chilled. This is very important to re-charge and boost your energy level and get ready for pursuing your dreams in life. You need to find your own way on how to control your emotions whenever somebody tries to make you feel sad, unhappy, or uncomfortable. There is a lot of information and guidance on the internet; however, I would advise you to find your own way to come out from any depression and anxiety caused but external factors. In my case, this was the SMILE. It's an easy word to say, but it's hard to maintain in tough situations. I managed to keep it all the time, even when others managed to make me upset. I can't stand to give them the opportunity to win, because I can't stand to be a loser, and I will never be one. My advice to you is to find your inside hidden power that can serve you during any tough and rough situation.

Lead by Example

Being a Muslim is not something you should be ashamed of. Be proud of yourself and your religion wherever you go and whoever you go with. You don't need to copy someone else to be appreciated by your colleagues. You don't need to copy somebody's speech patterns to be acceptable by others. You don't need to dress up like a celebrity to gain others' respect. You will never make it through, and you know why? Because it's all fake, and it's not the true you. Be yourself means making your own choice to dress the way you like; Jewish people put their Skullcap on, and Catholic nuns dress differently, and no one is blaming them. If you are wearing your Scarf, be proud of it. Be confident about yourself. I like to see more Muslim women on the stage giving inspirational and motivational speeches, Muslim women presenting programs in western societies, and Muslim women in big positions overseas because this will give a good impression to others. Muslim women are very intellectual, are very present in daily life, and can make a positive impact in the world too. We need to accept ourselves so others can accept us. Don't trap yourself by copying somebody who just looks cool and is popular. You will never get it unless you earn it. However, once you accept yourself and you accept who you are and where you come from, then people want to approach you, want to know you, get curious about you, and get curious about your personality. Never ever please somebody to gain respect, because respect is earned by hard work.

Help Others

"We cannot build our own future without helping others to build theirs."

-Bill Clinton

The best way to show the meaning of Islam is when you do something for others. It's about caring and sharing. We have an essential fact in Islam that says that if you want to succeed, you need to start by helping others. Some people may ask, "Why should I help them if they treat me bad? Why should I help them if they don't like me? Why should I help them if they put me down?" I've got one answer for all your questions: you are not like them. Don't treat people the way they treated you, because you are going to suffer. You are not like this. You grew up in a culture or religion where helping others is essential, where caring about others is eminent, so don't copy others. Be you. Don't change your roots and principles to please people. If they don't like you, it is their problem. If they hate you, it's their problem. If they don't treat you well, it's their problem. You are different, you are unique, and you are special. How does it look if you bake something and take it to work to share with your colleagues? How does it feel if you buy food for the homeless and give it to them? How does it sound if you take your unused items to charity to be used by somebody else who desperately needs it? It looks, feels, and sounds very good and shows your level of caring about others despite their appreciation it or no. I'm not talking about all people here. I'm talking about the minority of uneducated people who don't have any idea about Islam who are brainwashed and just go with the flow without thinking or making their own judgement. I do have many friends from different cultures (British, French, Italian, German, South African, Peruvian, Canadian …) who are amazing, who make your day with a smile, a word, or a gesture, and I'm sure you have the same as well. I'm so glad that I had the chance to get to know them and learn from them as often as they learn from me. It's a mutual friendship. We help, assist, and learn from each other.

The Truth of Islam

"Truth lifts the heart like water refreshes thirst."

                                                         -Unknown

Definition of Islam

If you search in Google about the meaning of Islam is:

Islam is an Arabic word meaning "submission" and, in the religious context, means "submission to the will of God". "Islam" is derived from the Arabic word "sal'm", which, literally, means peace. The religion itself demonstrates peace and tolerance.

"The face of terror is not the true faith of Islam. That's not what Islam is all about. Islam is peace. These terrorists don't represent peace. They represent evil and war."

                                        -George W. Bush

> "The word Islam means peace. The word Muslim means one who surrenders to God. But the press makes us seem like haters."
>
> -Muhammad Ali

As you can see, the word "Islam" originates from the word "peace". We grew up with that meaning, we believed in that meaning, and we live by this meaning. However, most people never had the chance to study Islam or learn about it properly, and unfortunately, they base their judgements on somebody else's experience. This is a total joke. Islam is a religion that encourages tolerance between peoples, encourages kindness between cultures, and encourages peace between religions. Islam accepts and respects other religions, and this is stated in Quran where Allah asked us to consider and respect other religions and respect their choices:

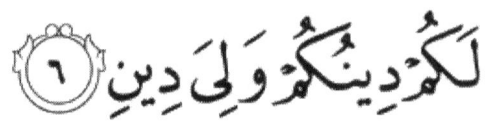

لَكُمْ دِينُكُمْ وَلِيَ دِينِ ﴿٦﴾

"For you is your religion, and for me is my religion."
(Surah Al-Khafirun, ayat 6)

Islam is a religion that teaches us how to take care of our neighbours no matter their religion, culture, background, or colour. It is a religion where children have been taught to take care of their parents once they get old. It is one where men are taught to take care of their families. And it is one in which we are taught to take care of animals, plants, and anything alive. People who have never visited any Muslim country or they had a bad experience with a Muslim person and are judging the whole Muslim community based on one bad experience or incident. I believe that is not fair.

Values of Islam

Islam is a religion that teaches us so many values in life which can serve us during our entire life. These lessons are key in any relationship between our parents, our children, friends, and other people. No matter what happens, we live with these values. This is how we grow up, and it's up to each person to implement it accordingly.

Tolerance

"The best of Islam is to behave with gentleness and tolerance."
  -Prophet Muhammad (*"peace be upon him"*)

This sentence explains it all. There is no need for us to feel ashamed when others talk about terrorists and blame it on Islam. This is wrong. We know that they must be talking about other religion or people who don't have any faith or don't believe in anything. Our religion is a pure symbol of tolerance between Muslim and other religions. There is no differentiation in Islam; all humans should be treated the same way, no matter where their country of origin, religion, colour, gender, culture, or any other criteria. It doesn't feel good whenever a terrorist act happens in London, Paris, or somewhere else and the blame falls directly on the Muslim community. We truly know that this person is not a Muslim or is just pretending to be a Muslim to make us look bad. Islam calls for peace between religions, for fairness between people, and for treating everyone fairly. Don't let what is happening affect your lifestyle or the way you contribute to the society. If people think you are terrorist because you are a Muslim, this is their point of view, but never let it become your reality.

Respecting others

"Whoever is not kind to the younger ones or does not respect the elders is not from my nation."
 -Prophet Muhammed (*"peace be upon him"*)

This is the way we grow up and this is how we've being thought in nurseries, schools and universities: to respect others including strangers, people with different religions, cultures, race, colour, and sex. This is how we interact with other people and deal with them no matter what they do to us; we don't respond on the same way. Islam teaches that our first object of respect should be our parents. Parents are the most valuable people to us; we need to take care of them in their old age in the same way they took care of us when we were little. Without our parents, we will never be here and be who we are today. Then we take care of our family (small or big), look after our kids, husband, wife, cousins, uncle, and so on. Family comes first under any circumstance. We support each other, help each other, and look after each other whenever it is needed. After that, we focus on friends and others. Islam teaches us to consider all people the same and not prefer any person over another, despite their differentiation. If you visit any Muslim country, you might notice that they welcome you, share their food with you, invite you to their houses, and treat you like one of them, like a member of the family. I remember one of my colleagues went to my home country (Morocco) because she was invited by a Moroccan friend to go with her. She was absolutely shocked by the way they treated her. She never felt like tourist or stranger to the country. She said, "Every day, they cook different food for me, they took me to see and discover new places, they never let me spend my money as they were paying for anything I want. The most amazing thing is when they took me to the Moroccan Hamam (like spa) they treated me like a queen, which I never felt the same even in my country."

For me, this is really a good thing to hear. However, this is not just in Morocco; it's all over Arabic countries. We like welcoming people, inviting them around, and making them feel comfortable and valuable. If you have an opportunity to visit an Arabic country (Morocco, Algeria, Tunisia, UAE, Egypt, or any other country), you are going to find the truth about Islam and the Muslim community by yourself. Islam is respect, and respect is one of the core-values of Islam. It is part of our daily life and culture and part of our daily conversation with our kids so, when they grow up, they can share the same principle with their kids and families.

Take Care and Be Kind

"If you expect the blessing from Allah, Be kind to his people."

-Abu Bakr

As you know, kindness is one of the most important values in Islam. It teaches us how to care about people in our daily life, not just on "Mother's Day", "Father's Day", or "Eid day". It's an ongoing task from birth to dead. As our parents gave us birth, food, shelter, and took us to school; when they become old, it's time to provide them with the similar thing instead of sending them to care houses. We take care of our parents before taking care of ourselves; we provide them with anything they need like they used to do for us. We are taught to never raise our voice to our parents and to continually show respect and kindness during our life. To be honest, I haven't seen this in Western society. I've seen people putting their parents in care houses; I've seen elderly people living by their own, and their kids never visit them. Some people are spending Christmas on their own. This is heartbreaking and not a part of our religion. The thing that hits me most is when I heard a TV advert claim that 2 million elderly people in Britain have no one to talk to. A woman said that she goes to the nearest shop every day to talk to people to not feel alone, which is very sad. I've seen it myself many times when shopping; a woman came towards my little daughter, Rania, who is a year old now, and started chatting with her and asking me questions about her, telling me about her stories when her kids were young. Now, they're all over 30 or 40 years old, and they don't see her much because they live abroad or in another city. They just don't have time to come around and are so busy with their lives.

However, in our culture, caring is a very important value our kids learn, especially as this will serve them during their life. Showing any kind of caring toward other people is important, and practicing it is essential. People like it when others look after them, care about their feelings, and care about their emotions. Just check on your neighbour while he or she is sick. This is counted as caring. Supporting your friends during hard times is kind of caring. Helping your team achieve their quarterly objectives and supporting them is kind of caring. Looking after your cat or dog is a kind of caring. There are so many examples to be used to teach or show other people how they can care or contribute to care about human beings. Any small gesture is counted, and guess what? You will feel very fulfilled after showing any kind of kindness to somebody else. This is internal satisfaction that cannot be experienced until you start practicing it. Just giving charity to a homeless will make you feel good, feel positive, and feel like you made a positive impact on this person's life. This is true. Your £1 can do so many things for him or her that you would never imagine.

My Journey to Self-Confidence

"Self-confidence is a superpower. Once you start to believe in yourself, magic starts happening."

-Unknown

Self-confidence is the ability to trust yourself in any difficult situation. Having a secured confidence in yourself will open doors and a future of success that were previously closed. However, not all people have the courage and confidence to trust themselves, especially if they were surrounded by other people who put them down all the time or people who didn't contribute to their self-growth. In this chapter, I will share a couple of points that allowed me to be who I am today and that helped me improve my personal and professional self. In my situation, I never imagined to be where I am now, and I never thought that what

I needed is a little push from myself and a bit of trust in my abilities and skills to reach my dreams. I believe you will be in the same situation where you need just a bit of motivation and confidence in yourself to be able to work on your dreams and achieve them. It's not easy to reach this level; however, it is still achievable with commitment and hard work.

Don't hide behind your excuses and try to stop yourself from becoming the best version of you. Facing problems is a normal part of life. I don't think life has meaning without problems in it. Do you? Problems are essential to sharpen your skills and make you stronger daily. Consider problems as a hard tool that you are going to accept and use during your life to overcome your obstacles and achieve your goals. Consider problems as iron that you need to heat first and mould it in the way to fit your use. During this chapter, you will discover more tips and advice in self-confidence from my own experience through different situations across different countries and which will make a difference in your life if you take them into serious consideration. You must do this enough to improve your personality, lifestyle, and achieve your goals.

Self-Care

"Self-care is giving the world the best of you, instead of what's left of you."

-Katie Reed

I'm really pleased to quote this sentence in here as this is a truthful aspect of our daily life. Self-care is being mindful and self-aware of your needs in a way that ensures you are being cared for by you. It's very important to take care of yourself first before looking after your kids, family, friends, colleagues, and the rest of the world as we say, "We can't pour from an empty cup." You cannot take care of your kids, play with them, and teach them good values if you don't have your own energy. You cannot deliver 100% in your job and meet the target if you don't feel you belong to your team and company. You cannot go out with your friends and have nice time together if you don't feel you can do

Self-Care

it or are able to do it. Self-care is an essential and important factor to survive daily life. It can be done through different ways, and it really depends on what you need to do to fulfil yourself. In my case, I have chosen a few things that allows me to feel cared for, loved, and fulfilled by myself and which helped me to overcome any hard situation in my life as well as stand strong as steel in front of wind. Physical self-care is one aspect; it can be anything that you like to do like going to the gym, walking in park, swimming, booking yourself a treatment day at the spa, getting manicures and pedicures, or anything that might affect your physical health. Emotional self-care is another aspect; yes, we need to care about our emotions as well as our physical selves. You might need to improve the feeling of belonging with your family, friends, or colleagues at work by simply getting closer to them and talking to them whenever you feel like it and express your feeling without be afraid or shy about it.

Psychological self-care is another aspect; in my opinion, this is the most neglected area that most people don't take it into consideration (including myself). Spiritual self-care is very important; this is not just practicing your religion, but this is when you get close to your inner human spirit and soul. There are many ways to practice this; you can do this by getting involved into charity activities, donating events, by spending more time in nature, meditating, and being grateful in your life. Professional self-care is yet another aspect; engaging in your professional life is essential, especially for those who are working and can make a big difference in their life. We spend more time at work than at home. This can be done in many ways such as chatting with your co-workers, inviting them for a drink after work, getting involved, and offering your help to find the perfect balance at work.

Think Positive

"A negative mind will never give you a positive life."

-Unknown

Switching your thoughts from negativity to positivity is a huge milestone for your self-development. It is not always easy to notice or catch yourself thinking negatively about something or someone. As we know, we can notice what's happening around us but not inside us. Help yourself to come out from any negative thoughts which will makes your situation even worse. Try to start your day with energy and positivity by doing some mediation or listening to your favourite music. Focus on the good things, no matter how small they are. This will stop your mind from building any negatively charged mental habits. Practice turning any failure in your life into a lesson instead of punishing yourself for not getting what you wanted to have. This is very important because failure is a part of life. No success is reached without failure. Stop listening to the little negative voice inside you. This is the time to start turning a situation to a lesson. Look around for positive friends, mentors, or co-workers. They are going to play a huge role in your life, on the way you think, on the way you behave, and, especially, on the way you react to any problems in your life. Positive minds aren't everywhere and aren't obvious to everyone. You need to look for them and try to learn from them as much as you can. If you didn't manage to get someone who might be able to help you think positively or switch the way you think, try to listen to videos and podcasts on the internet. Believe me; there are plenty there. Thanks to the amazing people who put their time and effort into producing such interesting videos, you can learn and grow from their knowledge and experiences, helping you make your own decisions.

I was and am still listening to motivational videos every morning before I go to work. It's become one of my daily routines and guess what? It is very effective in helping me overcome any stress or challenge I face at work. It helped me find a better way over any obstacle at work, in handling complaints and escalations, in motivating my team, and in changing the negative atmosphere to a positive one. It helped me become more honest with myself. People around me saw the changes and started questioning me. "Are you taking part in any meditation class? Are you part of motivational groups? Are you this? Are you that?" When I asked why they asked, I was surprised by their answers, because I never thought of it. It just came spontaneously, and it's work. I would strongly suggest the same thing if you want to take control of your life, take control of your thinking, and to improve your life. All you need is to change bad habits and start taking things seriously by planning and executing your objectives to reach your dreams. You have all the materials to be able to move on with your thinking and your life. The decision is in your hands. Take it, or you are going to lose yourself.

Set Small Goals to Achieve

"Set small goals along the way and don't be overwhelmed by the process."
                                        -Kara Goucher

The best way to make a difference in your life and reach your dreams is setting up a small and achievable goals. This is extremely helpful because you will notice you are working towards your dreams. You are starting to move forward, and you start to make a difference. Having a big dream is good but breaking it down into small steps is mandatory to be able to do it. I know many women who struggled to become what they dreamt of because they couldn't figure out how to achieve their big goals. They thought things happened overnight. They struggled with anxiety and depression due to failure. Why? Because there was no plan or guidance provided to achieve their goals, no steps or clear instructions to follow, and, by the end, they just gave up and forgot about their dreams. In my case, I wasn't sure how to start, especially since I have many goals and dreams to achieve. I feel a strong hunger, a need to succeed, and this book was one of my dreams. This particular dream started to become true not by chance but by the hard work I put into it and the constructive guidance I received. It helped me to understand the purpose of my book and how can I reach the end of the tunnel using the necessary tools. I started to prioritise my goals by filtering actions down to what can be achieved in a month, three months, six months, a year, and even five years. As you know, not all your dreams and goals can be done at once; that's why planning is key for success. the first thing you need to understand is what you want from yourself. What do you want to achieve? When do you want to reach it, and what are the necessary tools that can help you to achieve it?

Once you have a clear understanding and vision of all of the above questions, then you set up a time frame on each one and you stick to it as much as possible to familiarise yourself with self-discipline.

Start writing down your plans, ideas, and guidance, anything that might help you achieve what you want. Put it in your notebook, and I strongly advise you to have one. I've seen people just talking randomly about their objectives and plans, but they have no clue on how to do them or when to accomplish them. The worst bit is they never write them down, so they talk about them today and forgot about half of them tomorrow. Write down any idea that might be useful to you. Engage with the right people. This means people that can add a value to you dreams, who can help you achieve what you want, not people who are going to waste your time and put you down or suck your energy for nothing, as we call them "energy vampires". Surround yourself with the right people to be able to move forward; if you cannot find anyone, stick to yourself. You are the best company for yourself. The important thing is the finish line. It doesn't matter if you cross it by yourself or with the help of somebody else as long as you make it happen, and you make it real.

Be Grateful

"Gratitude opens the doors to ... the power, the wisdom, the creativity of the universe. You open the doors through gratitude."
-Deepak Chopra

Gratitude is an act of appreciation of something or to someone.
As defined on Google

Gratitude should be part of your life if you want to make a difference in your future. It plays a huge role in understanding and acknowledging that what you have is precious and that most people don't have the chance to have it. I'm always grateful to God for what He gives me every day of my life. I thank God every day for being alive and allowing me another day where

I can make difference in my life and in someone else's life too. I thank God for letting me breathe without having any issues or problems, for my eyes so I can see the beauty of the world, for my ears so I can hear the sound of nature, for my hands so I'm able to touch things and reach anything without any difficulties, to walk without any wheelchair or crutches, and, finally, I thank God for having a normal body without any diseases. We should all be grateful for what we have and appreciate the value of things under our control. The grass always looks greener on the other side. We keep looking at things that others have, and we forget about the value of the things we have.

Gratitude should be a part of your daily prayers, daily meditation, and daily routine. If you don't appreciate what you have now, you will never value what you going to have in the future. This is a very important attitude to be taught to our children as well. They need to value the food on table, the roof over of their heads, and whatever they have instead of complaining and whining about things that they don't have. Once you reach a state where you appreciate being alive, when gratitude becomes as essential as drinking water or eating food, then, welcome to the new you. At that time, you will start to see a meaning in everything around you, and you'll start to value everything you have and make the best use of it. Being grateful is being thankful for the smallest thing you have. It is recognizing its worth.

Empower Yourself with Knowledge

This picture represents how Islam is encouraging women to learn and educate themselves. It shows that there is no difference between her and men when it comes to gaining knowledge. The first and oldest established university in the world is al-Qarawiyyin university based in Fes, Morocco and was founded by a woman, Fatima al Fihri. This is a big statement that shows the world the importance of women in Islam and how they can make a huge difference in the world.

> "Knowledge is power, and you need power in this world. You need as many advantages as you can get."
>
> -Ellen Degeneres

Empower Yourself with Knowledge 121

> **RIGHT TO EDUCATION**
> **1821** UNDER WESTERN RULE
> **841** UNDER ISLAMIC RULE
>
> The fight for education for women saw the emergence of the first university for women in the US in 1821. In 1841 women were formally allowed to teach in Universities.
>
> It was Fatima al Fihriyya under the Khilafah that built the first university during 841 CE in Morocco. Science along with other various Subjects were taught in the University.
>
> **WOMEN AGAINST OPPRESSION - LIBERATION THROUGH ISLAM**

Knowledge is an essential factor to success. If you want to succeed in life and reach your dreams, you need to gain the necessary knowledge and experience to improve and grow yourself. I would recommend any woman who want to progress in her life begin by educating herself. It's not easy.

It will never be easy, but with your perseverance and hard work, you will be able to be in where you want to be. In my case, hard work was essential to progress and reach my dreams. It was a lot of sleepless nights. Many times, I felt tired and exhausted and thought of quieting. Thank God my "why" was bigger than my excuses, and, with the support of my husband, it is why you see this book out in the market. Keep reading books as much as you can; reading is one of the ways in which you will gain more knowledge and information about any subject you want to study or improve on in your life.

Spend your time researching to have more information and skills in any area you want to improve. You will then notice the difference in yourself. You will have more confidence in yourself while talking about any specific topic or when working on any project. You are going to make difference in your workplace, your family, and your surroundings. Once you start feeling the difference, you will be hungry to learn and acquire more skills. This is the start of a new you. This is when you are going to see a new and best version of yourself. Nothing is difficult in this world if you put your full focus in it. *Everything is Figureoutable* is an interesting book written by Marie Forleo that explains that, as human beings, we can reach whatever we want in this life. We simply need to obtain the right knowledge and skills as well as have a strong desire and hunger to be successful.

Have a Vision for Your Dream

"Vison get the dream started."
-Emmitt Smith

Without a clear vision for your dreams, you won't be successful. It is important for anyone to have a vision in place before starting to work on their dreams. In my case, I had a vision about all my dreams, and I'm trying very hard to accomplish one before starting another one. in this case I don't feel overwhelmed even though they're all important to me. One of my biggest dreams is the be the Ambassador of Muslim women in Western society, meaning I want to talk to others about our religion, our cultures, about women and how can we make a difference, and about how we can add value to where we live.

Have a Vision for Your Dream

I would like to support any woman, regardless of her religion, culture, or race in achieving her dreams, to feel that she is productive, to be herself, and to feel that she belongs. It wasn't easy for me to integrate into UK; everything is different when you compare other European countries to Morocco. Despite the hard time I've being through since I came to UK, especially when you see people underestimate you because you are wearing a Scarf, it doesn't take anything from me anymore. Some people even feel that the fact that English is not your first language, you're not fit to take a decent position within the company. That is ludicrous. Of course, I wasn't fluent in English when I moved to UK, because English is my third language. I have a noticeable accent, because my mother language is Arabic. I believe any English, French, Spanish-speaking person trying to speak Arabic would have an accent too. I've seen many French, Spanish, or English-speaking people who live in Morocco and are trying to speak in a Moroccan accent to feel like locals or that they belong to the society. They talk with an accent, and no one looks at them like it's something disgusting or that they must talk properly. Well done to them, because they are trying hard to speak like us and get involved within our culture.

Why don't we see the same thing in Western culture? Why we don't see support from others like we do in our countries? I'm not blaming everyone of course. I've met incredible people who helped me progress in my professional life, who supported me during my learning stage, and who provided and are still providing me with all kinds of assistance to be where I am today. I would like to thank them one by one. Having a vision about what you want to achieve in your life will facilitate the way to it. Try to know people who might play a big role in improving your situation, keep learning every day, and keep gaining new skills that will serve you one day whenever you need it. The first step to success is to have the hunger for success, to have the desire for success, and, especially, to have the persistence and a vision for success.

To all women:

You stop talking yourself down and start embracing the "flawsome" woman that you already are — fabulous and fallible, brilliant and blundering, innately lovable and wholly imperfect — all at the same time.

You stop letting self-doubt call the shots and start acting with the confidence you wish you had.

You stop dwelling about what you don't have and start making the most of what you've got. (Which is plenty!)

You stop punishing yourself for past mistakes and start applying their lessons to live more deeply and choose more wisely.

You stop thinking about what you'd like to say and start having the brave conversations you've been putting off.

You stop saying yes to keep people happy and you start saying no to anything that doesn't align with the boldest vision for your life.

You stop waiting for permission or perfection and start putting yourself out there, ready to fail forward and forge a bigger life rich in meaning, connection and contribution.

-Margie Warrell

Printed in Great Britain
by Amazon